D1538199

A Guide to
AMERICAN STATES

District of Columbia

THE NATION'S CAPITAL

MEDIA ENHANCED BOOKS

AV2 BY WEIGL

ADDED VALUE • AUDIO VISUAL

www.av2books.com

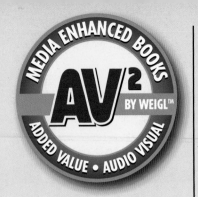

AV² provides enriched content that supplements and complements this book. Weigl's AV² books strive to create inspired learning and engage young minds in a total learning experience.

Your AV² Media Enhanced books come alive with...

Audio
Listen to sections of the book read aloud.

Key Words
Study vocabulary, and complete a matching word activity.

Go to **www.av2books.com**, and enter this book's unique code.

Video
Watch informative video clips.

Quizzes
Test your knowledge.

BOOK CODE

N 5 9 8 7 8

Embedded Weblinks
Gain additional information for research.

Slide Show
View images and captions, and prepare a presentation.

AV² by Weigl brings you media enhanced books that support active learning.

Try This!
Complete activities and hands-on experiments.

... and much, much more!

Published by AV² by Weigl
350 5th Avenue, 59th Floor
New York, NY 10118
Website: www.av2books.com   www.weigl.com

Library of Congress Cataloging-in-Publication Data

Thomas, William, 1947-
 District of Columbia / William Thomas.
   p. cm. -- (A guide to American states)
Includes index.
ISBN 978-1-61690-821-8 (hardcover : alk. paper) -- ISBN 978-1-61690-456-2 (online)
1. Washington (D.C.)--Juvenile literature. I. Title.
F194.3.T46 2011
975.3--dc22
                        2011018321

Printed in the United States of America in North Mankato, Minnesota

052011
WEP180511

Project Coordinator Jordan McGill
Art Director Terry Paulhus

Contents

Washington's celebrated cherry blossoms bloom in the spring. Many of the city's cherry trees are near the Jefferson Memorial, which honors the nation's third president, Thomas Jefferson.

Introduction

Washington, D.C. is the capital city of the United States. It is where the president lives and where Congress meets to make the nation's laws. Dozens of **federal** government departments and agencies have their headquarters in the city.

The *D.C.* in Washington's name stands for "District of Columbia." The name *Columbia*, which comes from Christopher Columbus, was commonly used after the American Revolution to refer to the United States. The district was created more than 200 years ago as a home for the federal government. The city was named for George Washington, the first U.S. president. In the beginning, the city took up only a small part of the district's land, but it has grown over time.

The White House, 1600 Pennsylvania Avenue, is the official residence of the president.

The Lincoln Memorial holds a larger-than-life statue of President Abraham Lincoln, who led the nation through the Civil War.

The district has beautiful parks, a famous zoo, and many **monuments** and historic buildings. Visitors can tour the White House, where the president lives. Washington's many museums have collections that include dinosaurs, paintings by the world's greatest artists, the Wright Brothers' first airplane, and boxing gloves used by heavyweight fighter Muhammed Ali.

Interstate Highways 95 and 495 make a circle around Washington. **Residents** call this highway ring "the Beltway." The city's streets and broad avenues come together at traffic circles found throughout the district. Instead of driving, many Washingtonians use the Metro, one of the world's finest subway systems. The Washington area is served by three major airports. They are Ronald Reagan Washington National Airport, Dulles International Airport, and Baltimore/Washington International Thurgood Marshall Airport.

Where Is the District of Columbia?

Washington, D.C., is in the Mid-Atlantic region of the United States. It is a roughly diamond-shaped area of land located between northern Virginia and central Maryland.

The District of Columbia is not part of any state. Its creation began in 1790, when Congress passed a bill that set aside land for a capital. The land, which was on both sides of the Potomac River, came from the states of Virginia and Maryland. At the time, it was called the Territory of Columbia. The word *territory* was later changed to "district."

A long open and tree-lined area called the National Mall stretches westward from the Capitol, where Congress meets.

Washington's location was a **compromise**. When the United States was formed, New York City was the capital. Then Philadelphia became the capital. The Northern states wanted the capital to remain in the North. Southern states feared that having the capital in the North would lead to ending slavery. An agreement was finally reached. The Southern states supported a financial plan wanted by the North. In return the nation's capital would move to a location that was considered part of the South.

The district is not very big. It covers just 69 square miles, but it used to be larger. In 1846, at the request of residents in the part of the district south of the Potomac, that part was returned to Virginia. All of the land now in Washington, D.C., was once part of Maryland. Today, Washington is a bustling, hard-working city. The city and its suburbs make up what is called the Metro Area, which is home to 5.5 million people.

Washington traffic can be very heavy. More than 200,000 vehicles use the Beltway every day.

Mapping the District of Columbia

Maryland surrounds the District of Columbia to the north, east, and southeast. On the southwest side of the city, the Potomac River separates it from Virginia. The Anacostia River flows through the southeast part of the city.

Washington is divided into four parts called quadrants. They are northwest, northeast, southwest, and southeast. These quadrants are usually abbreviated as NW, NE, SW, and SE, respectively. They intersect at the Capitol.

Sites and Symbols

OFFICIAL SEAL
District of Columbia

OFFICIAL FLAG
District of Columbia

OFFICIAL TREE
Scarlet Oak

OFFICIAL FLOWER
American Beauty Rose

OFFICIAL BIRD
Wood Thrush

Nickname The Nation's Capital, The Capital City

Motto *Justitia Omnibus* ("Justice for All")

Song "Washington," words and music by Jimmie Dodd

Entered the Union July 16, 1790

Population (2010 Census) 601,723

NATION'S CAPITAL

On July 16, 1790, President George Washington signed the Residence Act. This measure passed by Congress called on the president to select a site on the Potomac River for the nation's capital. He chose a site only about 16 miles north of his Mount Vernon home in Virginia. The law also gave him the authority to appoint three people as commissioners to oversee the site's development. Ten years later, in 1800, Washington officially became the nation's capital. By that time, John Adams was the president.

Triadelphia Res.

Columbia

MARYLAND

Redland

Olney

Rocky Gorge Res.

Gaithersburg

270

Aspen Hill

Laurel

95

Rockville

Colesville

South Laurel

North Bethesda

Beltsville

Patuxent R.

Potomac

Silver Spring

495

Bethesda

Adelphi

Greenbelt

Potomac R.

College Park

Chillum

VIRGINIA

Tysons Corner

66

★ **Washington D.C.**

Arlington

Coral Hills

Jefferson

Forestville

495

Annandale

Hillcrest Heights

Lincolnia

395

Alexandria

495

Camp Springs

Springfield

Rose Hill

Oxon Hill

95

Groveton

Clinton

N

Map Scale

0

20 Miles

United States

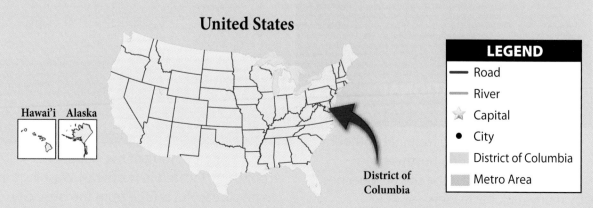

Hawai'i Alaska

District of Columbia

LEGEND

— Road

— River

★ Capital

• City

District of Columbia

Metro Area

The Land

Washington, D.C. is part of two geographic regions, the **piedmont** and the coastal plain. The northwestern part of the district is in the piedmont. This higher, hilly land stretches westward to the Appalachian Mountains. Most of Washington is on the coastal plain. This land is generally flat, with a few low hills.

Water is Washington's most distinctive feature. Rock Creek and the Anacostia River flow through the city. The broad Potomac River forms the district's southwestern border.

WASHINGTON NATIONAL CATHEDRAL

Completed in 1912, the National Cathedral stands in Washington's northwest quadrant. It has been the site of speeches by many national leaders.

U.S. NATIONAL ARBORETUM

The trees and flowers of the National Arboretum, located in northeast Washington, create a peaceful refuge from the busy city.

REFLECTING POOL

The western extension of the National Mall features a 2,029-foot-long reflecting pool, which stretches from the Lincoln Memorial almost to the Washington Monument.

THEODORE ROOSEVELT ISLAND

A footbridge from the Virginia shore leads to Theodore Roosevelt Island, a memorial park in the Potomac River honoring the 26th U.S. president.

I DIDN'T KNOW THAT!

The highest land point in Washington is Fort Reno Park's Reno Hill in the city's northwest quadrant. It is 409 feet above sea level. The lowest point is on the Potomac River, which is barely above sea level.

Rock Creek carved a deep ravine as it flowed to the Potomac through what is now Washington, D.C. Today, much of the land along the creek is a forested park.

About 15 miles west of Washington, at the Great Falls of the Potomac, the river drops more than 75 feet into a rocky gorge.

Although Washington usually does not get very severe winters, occasional heavy snowfalls blanket the city in white.

Climate

ashington, D.C. has a temperate climate with four distinct seasons. Summers in the district are well known for being warm and humid. The average maximum temperature in July is 88.3° Fahrenheit, and the average minimum is 70.1° F. Winters can be cold. The average maximum temperature in January is 42.5° F, and the average minimum is 27.3° F.

Each year the district usually gets about 15 inches of snow. Powerful storms called Nor'easters have sometimes dumped more than 10 inches of snow on Washington in a single day. Average annual precipitation, including both rain and snow, is about 40 inches.

The highest temperature ever recorded in Washington was 106° F, on August 6, 1918, and July 20, 1930. The lowest was –15° F, on February 11, 1899.

Average Monthly Temperatures in Washington, D.C.

What aspects of Washington's location account for the variation in temperature over the course of a year?

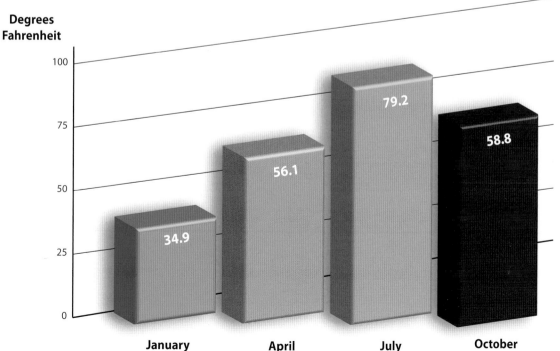

Degrees Fahrenheit

- January: 34.9
- April: 56.1
- July: 79.2
- October: 58.8

Natural Resources

Many American states have forests for timber, mountains with coal or other minerals, fertile plains for farming, or oil beneath the land. The tiny District of Columbia never had many natural resources. Long ago, farmers in the area raised cattle and grew corn and tobacco. But most of the land on which Washington would be built was too low and swampy for large-scale farming.

The Tidal Basin was built in 1897 to help prevent flooding by the Potomac River. Today, it is considered one of the most beautiful areas of Washington, D.C.

A small wetland at the National Museum of the American Indian re-creates an environment that centuries ago was common in the Washington area.

In 1632, an English explorer in the area told how the Indians caught large numbers of sturgeon in the Anacostia River. Since then, fish have largely disappeared from the Anacostia because of overfishing and water pollution.

The district's greatest natural resource was, and still is, the Potomac River. Although its water must be carefully cleaned, the river provides most of the city's drinking water. Groups such as the Potomac Conservancy are working to protect the river, its wildlife, and the wetlands around it.

Plants

Every spring, people come from around the world to see the cherry blossoms in Washington. The cherry trees were given to the city in 1912 by the people of Japan. Today, thousands of them grow near the Tidal Basin and the Jefferson Memorial.

While the cherry trees are renowned, the area around the Tidal Basin is not the only place in the city to see flowering plants. The U.S. National Arboretum, a park in the northeast part of Washington, has azaleas, dogwoods, magnolias, and many other plants that flower.

Most of the trees in Washington were cut down when the city was being built. President Thomas Jefferson helped to restore trees to the area. He had poplar trees planted along Pennsylvania Avenue, between the White House and the Capitol. They were eventually replaced with elm and linden trees. Today, oaks, maples, sycamores, and other trees also grow along the streets and in the city's parks.

RED MAPLE TREE

Washington's red maples put on a spectacular show in the fall, when their leaves become fiery bright.

JACK-IN-THE-PULPIT

Wetland plants such as the jack-in-the-pulpit grow in some areas by the Anacostia River.

LINDEN TREE

A favorite shade tree, the linden is also known for its distinctive fragrance.

AZALEA

Azaleas are flowering shrubs that bloom for a few weeks each spring. They grow well in the Washington, D.C., area.

An estimated 35 percent of Washington's area is beneath leafy tree branches, or a "tree canopy," as seen from above. This is largely because of the contribution of such wooded areas as Rock Creek Park and Fort DuPont Park. Authorities are working to raise the figure to 40 percent by planting elms and other trees.

The cherry trees along the Tidal Basin are all ornamental. They do not bear fruit. In 1938, a group of women feared that some of the district's cherry trees would be cut down when the Jefferson Memorial was built. The women chained themselves to the trees until they were promised that the trees would be safe.

Animals

Deer and herds of bison, or buffalo, once roamed the land that is now Washington, D.C. The buffalo disappeared long ago, but deer are still found in a few areas of the city. Squirrels, chipmunks, opossums, raccoons, skunks, and foxes also make their homes in the city's parks and wooded areas.

In recent years, environmental groups have worked to clean up the waters of the Potomac and Anacostia rivers. Wildlife has returned, including catfish, sunfish, shad, and bass. Great blue herons nest near the riverbanks.

President Theodore Roosevelt once listed 90 different kinds of birds that he saw from the White House or elsewhere in Washington. About the same number can be found today, including thrushes, warblers, finches, blue jays, mockingbirds, and orioles. The city is also home to many pigeons and seagulls.

WHITE-TAILED DEER

A number of white-tailed deer make their homes in Rock Creek Park and nearby wooded areas.

BALD EAGLE

The bald eagle is the symbol of the United States. These majestic birds nest at several sites in the Washington area, especially in parks and along riverbanks.

GRAY SQUIRREL

Washington's parks boast an abundance of gray squirrels. In warmer months the squirrels store food for the winter by burying it, sometimes in hundreds of different places.

NORTHERN CARDINAL

Found in Washington and throughout the eastern United States, northern cardinals are famous for their bright red color, which actually occurs only in the males.

I DIDN'T KNOW THAT!

In 1999, a family of beavers started chopping down the celebrated cherry trees by the Tidal Basin. The animals were trapped and then set free far away from the capital.

Dolley Madison, the wife of President James Madison, often greeted White House visitors with her pet parrot sitting on her shoulder.

President Calvin Coolidge had a pet raccoon, named Rebecca, that ran loose in the White House.

Two pandas are among the biggest attractions at Washington's National Zoo. The male is named Tian Tian, which means "more, more." The female is Mei Xiang, meaning "beautiful fragrance."

Tourism

More than 15 million people visit Washington, D.C. every year. Some tour the White House, the Capitol, or the Supreme Court. Many go to art galleries or the museums of the Smithsonian Institution. People stroll along the National Mall, ride an elevator to the top of the Washington Monument, walk through the Lincoln Memorial and Jefferson Memorial, or stand quietly before the black stone walls of the Vietnam Veterans Memorial.

The animals at the National Zoo are a big tourist attraction. The city's professional sports teams are popular with both tourists and residents. Annual events such as the Cherry Blossom Festival in spring, July Fourth celebrations, and the lighting of the National Christmas Tree bring large numbers of visitors to Washington.

WASHINGTON MONUMENT

Honoring the first president, the Washington Monument is located on the National Mall, directly south of the White House. More than 555 feet high, it took 36 years to build.

SUPREME COURT

The Supreme Court, the highest court in the nation, did not get its own building until 1935. Today, visitors can take a self-guided tour that includes part of the building, and they can listen to lectures about the Supreme Court.

LIBRARY OF CONGRESS

The Library of Congress has the most books of any library in the world. Its collections also include historic maps, photographs, and newspapers.

FDR MEMORIAL

Franklin Delano Roosevelt was the country's longest-serving president. The memorial honoring him features sculptures showing scenes from his presidency and even his pet dog Fala.

The National Air and Space Museum is the most popular museum in the world. It averages more than 9 million visitors a year.

The Washington Monument was built of white stone, except for the very top of it. That is made of aluminum. This metal was very expensive when the monument was completed in 1884.

The Vietnam Veterans Memorial was designed by a 21-year old college student named Maya Ying Lin. The names of all 58,000 Americans killed or missing in the Vietnam War are carved into its walls.

Industry

Government and tourism are the two biggest types of industry in Washington. More than one-fourth of the district's working residents are employed by government. City government workers include schoolteachers, police officers, firefighters, and trash collectors. The federal government employs tens of thousands of people. They work at departments and agencies such as the State Department, the Internal Revenue Service, the Department of Health and Human Services, the Federal Aviation Administration, and the Federal Bureau of Investigation.

Industries in the District of Columbia
Value of Goods and Services in Millions of Dollars

Many private companies in Washington depend on money spent by tourists. In what industries shown in the pie chart is tourism an important factor in the size of the industry?

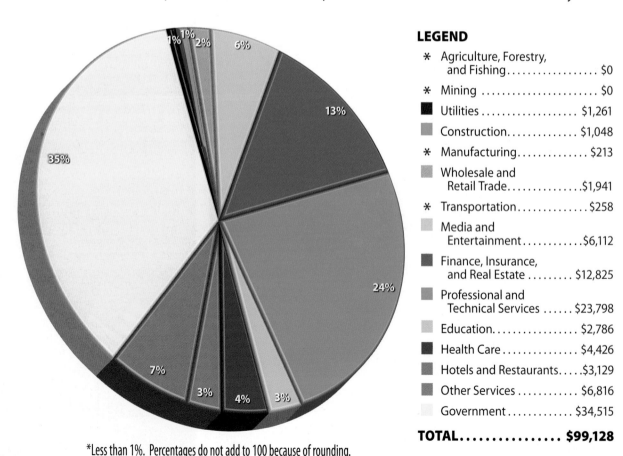

LEGEND

*	Agriculture, Forestry, and Fishing	$0
*	Mining	$0
■	Utilities	$1,261
■	Construction	$1,048
*	Manufacturing	$213
■	Wholesale and Retail Trade	$1,941
*	Transportation	$258
■	Media and Entertainment	$6,112
■	Finance, Insurance, and Real Estate	$12,825
■	Professional and Technical Services	$23,798
■	Education	$2,786
■	Health Care	$4,426
■	Hotels and Restaurants	$3,129
■	Other Services	$6,816
■	Government	$34,515

TOTAL **$99,128**

*Less than 1%. Percentages do not add to 100 because of rounding.

Tourism is the capital's second-largest category of industry. Hotels, restaurants, tour-bus companies, gift shops, souvenir stands, theaters, and car-rental companies are all part of the tourism industry. Nearly all tourist businesses are private. That means they are owned and operated by groups of people rather than the government. In Washington, many other private businesses help the government and government workers do their jobs. These businesses include law firms, banks, and real estate agencies.

Ronald Reagan Washington National Airport, located right across the Potomac in Virginia, is the airport closest to the center of Washington. Many members of Congress and other federal officials regularly use the airport to travel on government business.

Goods and Services

There is very little manufacturing in Washington, but the industry that produces the most goods is probably printing. Visitors stand in long lines to watch paper money being made at the Bureau of Engraving and Printing. The Bureau also prints stamps, identification cards, and invitations to events at the White House.

The Government Printing Office, or GPO, is another large operation. Its main plant is the largest information-processing, printing, and distribution facility in the world. The GPO prints the national **budget**, income tax forms, and safety regulations. It has even done a comic book about a character named Squeaks. The book is about the history of printing.

Billions of dollars worth of paper currency roll off the presses of the Bureau of Engraving and Printing every year.

Nearly all types of jobs in government and tourism are service work. Service workers do things for people rather than make things. Doctors, auto mechanics, school teachers, college professors, plumbers, lawyers, and gardeners are all service workers.

Influence is also a service, and many companies and other organizations in Washington are in the influence, or lobbying, business. They work to change or support government policies and laws. The National Wildlife Federation, for example, tries to convince the government to take actions that protect wild animals and their habitats. The American Association of Retired Persons seeks ways that the government can do more to help older people. The U.S. Chamber of Commerce attempts to get the government to set policies that help businesses.

Colleges and universities employ many people in Washington, D.C. Georgetown University, the city's oldest, admitted its first students in 1792.

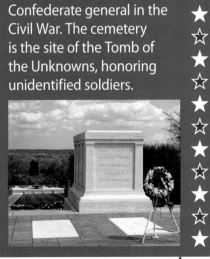

American Indians

When the first Europeans arrived, the largest American Indian group in the area north of the Potomac River was the Piscataway. South of the river the main Indian group was the Powhatan.

The Indians built villages surrounded by high wooden fences. Their homes were fairly large. They were built from tree limbs, bark, and reed mats. More than one family often lived in a house. There was a central fire pit in each one, with a hole above to let out the smoke.

Men hunted deer, bear, and turkeys, and they caught fish in the rivers. In spring, they cleared fields near their villages for planting. Women grew crops such as corn, squash, beans, and tobacco. They also wove baskets and made clothing.

Traditional foods of the Indians who lived in the region of present-day Washington included squash, seeds, nuts, beans, mushrooms, and berries.

English explorers and settlers arrived in the area in the early 1600s. Although the English and the American Indians sometimes cooperated, relations between them were never good. European diseases such as measles and smallpox killed thousands of American Indians. Fighting broke out as more settlers moved onto Indian lands. Bloody battles were fought, with victories by both sides. The Piscataway and Powhatan were also attacked by Indians from the north called Susquehannocks. When the English arrived, a few thousand American Indians lived in the area that is now Washington, D.C. By 1700, only a few hundred remained.

The National Museum of the American Indian is devoted to the history, customs, and crafts of native cultures of the western hemisphere.

Thirteen thousand years ago, people called Paleo-Indians were already living in the area that is now Washington, D.C.

The word *Potomac* comes from the Piscataway name "Pa-ta-wo-me-ke." Some experts believe that it means "trading place."

In the mid-1990s, thousands of objects were found during construction of a road near the mouth of Rock Creek. They included a comb and jewelry made from shark's teeth dating from about 1,400 years ago.

A re-creation of a traditional Powhatan Indian village can be seen today at Jamestown Settlement in Virginia.

In 1634 a group of English colonists landed along the Potomac, in what is now Maryland, to begin settlements in the area.

Explorers

E nglish explorer John Smith came to Virginia with a group of families from England in 1607. They established a village called Jamestown about 120 miles south of the future site of Washington, D.C. Jamestown was the first permanent English settlement in North America. The next year, 1608, Smith sailed north. He explored the Potomac as far as the present site of Washington and made a map of the area. More English families arrived in 1619. They settled on the James River, north of Jamestown, in a place they called Berkeley Hundred.

In 1634, another group of English settlers came to the region. They were turned away by American Indians near the future site of Washington, and they finally established a village on a branch of the Potomac near where the river empties into Chesapeake Bay. That settlement became the present-day town of St. Mary's City, Maryland. In the following years, the English settlers moved north, starting farms and villages in the area that would become the District of Columbia.

Timeline of Settlement

Early Exploration and Settlement

1608 John Smith explores and maps the Potomac River and Chesapeake Bay area.

1632 King Charles I of England gives the province of Maryland to Cecil Calvert, Lord Baltimore.

1634 English settlers start a settlement in Maryland.

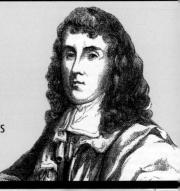

New Towns and Revolution

1749 Alexandria is founded in Virginia, across the Potomac from present-day Washington.

1751 The Maryland Assembly authorizes the establishment of Georgetown, a port on the Potomac that eventually becomes part of Washington.

1776 The 13 American colonies declare independence from Great Britain.

A New Country and Civil War

1790 Congress passes a law calling for the establishment of a new U.S. capital on the Potomac River.

1800 The U.S. government moves from Philadelphia to Washington.

1814 British troops burn the Capitol, the White House, and other public buildings in Washington during the War of 1812.

1861–1865 During the Civil War, a number of important battles are fought in northern Virginia, close to Washington, D.C. Many federal troops are stationed in the city to protect it from invasion.

1865 The Civil War ends, and President Abraham Lincoln is assassinated in Washington.

Early Settlers

T he land that George Washington chose for the national capital was largely forest and swamps, with a few small settlements and farms. Construction of the new federal city began in 1792. Congress met in the city for the first time on November 17, 1800.

Map of Settlements and Resources in the Early District of Columbia

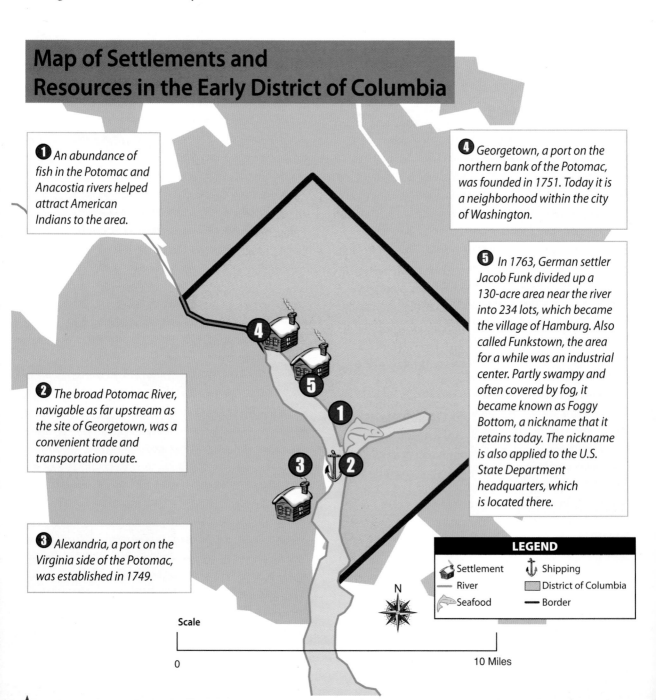

1 An abundance of fish in the Potomac and Anacostia rivers helped attract American Indians to the area.

4 Georgetown, a port on the northern bank of the Potomac, was founded in 1751. Today it is a neighborhood within the city of Washington.

5 In 1763, German settler Jacob Funk divided up a 130-acre area near the river into 234 lots, which became the village of Hamburg. Also called Funkstown, the area for a while was an industrial center. Partly swampy and often covered by fog, it became known as Foggy Bottom, a nickname that it retains today. The nickname is also applied to the U.S. State Department headquarters, which is located there.

2 The broad Potomac River, navigable as far upstream as the site of Georgetown, was a convenient trade and transportation route.

3 Alexandria, a port on the Virginia side of the Potomac, was established in 1749.

LEGEND

Settlement		Shipping
River		District of Columbia
Seafood		Border

N

Scale

0

10 Miles

Washington, which did not yet include the port of Georgetown, had about 3,000 residents by 1800, including construction workers and slaves. Oliver Wolcott, Jr., then secretary of the Treasury, said, "There are few houses in any one place, and most of them small, miserable huts." Pennsylvania Avenue, the street connecting the White House and the Capitol, was described as "a muddy trail." The city grew quickly. By 1820, more than 13,000 people lived there. By 1860, just before the Civil War began, the population had grown to 75,000. In 1900, a century after the federal government moved to Washington, the city's population was more than 275,000.

Washington was a small town in its early days. In 1800 the number of people working for the federal government was only about 130.

I DIDN'T KNOW THAT!

French architect Pierre L'Enfant was picked by George Washington to design the capital city. L'Enfant wanted to put the Capitol in the center of the city, with wide avenues going out from it like spokes on a wheel. In accordance with his plan, the Capitol was built on a low rise then called Jenkins Hill. Today it is known as Capitol Hill. Members of Congress often say they work "on the hill."

Disagreements about the project led to the firing of L'Enfant. An African American astronomer and surveyor named Benjamin Banneker played a key role in laying out Washington's streets, using many of L'Enfant's ideas.

British soldiers burned much of Washington during the War of 1812. Stories say that the president's house was painted white to cover the burns and smoke stains. People began calling it the White House.

In central Washington, most streets going north and south are numbered, such as 7th Street. Most of those running east and west are lettered, such as C Street. The diagonal avenues are named for states, such as Pennsylvania Avenue.

Notable People

Many people born or raised in Washington, D.C., have gained renown for outstanding achievements in their chosen fields. They include leading activists and reformers, as well as prominent figures in the arts, media, and sports.

**CLARA BARTON
(1821–1912)**

A Massachusetts-born teacher and nurse, Barton moved to Washington, D.C., in 1854. During the Civil War she played a leading role in providing food for the troops and aid to the wounded, gaining fame as the "Angel of the Battlefield." The founder and first president of the American Red Cross, she established the first U.S. chapter of the organization in 1881.

**DUKE ELLINGTON
(1899–1974)**

Born in Washington, D.C., composer, pianist, and bandleader Duke Ellington blended jazz, blues, gospel, and classical styles into what he called simply "American music." He wrote more than 1,000 songs and other musical works, including "Mood Indigo" and "It Don't Mean a Thing (If It Ain't Got That Swing)." After his death, he was awarded a Pulitzer Prize.

CONNIE CHUNG (1946–)

An award-winning TV news reporter and broadcaster, Chung was born and raised in Washington. From 1993 to 1995 she was coanchor of the *CBS Evening News*. She was the first Asian American, and only the second woman, to be a news anchor at a major network. She has also been a coanchor of *20/20* and has hosted other news programs.

SAMUEL L. JACKSON (1948–)

Born in Washington, D.C, Jackson is best-known for his movie roles, but he has also acted on TV and on stage. In addition, he has worked as a producer. His many movies include *Do the Right Thing, Jurassic Park, Pulp Fiction,* two of the *Iron Man* movies, and three *Star Wars* films. Jackson was active in civil rights protests in the 1960s.

PETE SAMPRAS (1971–)

Sampras, born in Washington, D.C., began playing tennis with an old racket he found in his basement at the age of three. He went on to become one of the greatest players of all time. Sampras won a total of 14 Grand Slam singles championships and many other tournaments around the world. He retired in 2003.

I DIDN'T KNOW THAT!

Ann Beattie (1947–), born in Washington, D.C., is a short story writer and novelist. She has published such critically praised story collections as *Distortions, Secrets & Surprises*, and *Follies*. Her first novel, *Chilly Scenes of Winter*, was made into a motion picture. She was elected a member of the American Academy of Arts and Letters in 1993.

Sugar Ray Leonard (1956–), who grew up in Washington, D.C., and a Maryland suburb, was one of the greatest boxers of all time. He won an Olympic gold medal in 1976, and he went on to earn more than $100 million in prize money in his professional career. He captured world titles in five different weight classes.

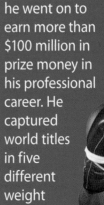

Population

About 600,000 people live in Washington, making it the 27th most populous city in the country. The greater metropolitan area, which includes parts of Virginia and Maryland, has about 5.5 million residents. For many years the district's population was declining. In recent years, the city has experienced slow growth. Washington's birth rate is 15.4 births per 1,000 people. That is higher than the national average of 14.0 births per 1,000 people.

Historically, Washington has had a large African American population. Today, African Americans make up 54 percent of the city's residents. People of European ancestry account for more than 40 percent of the population, and Asian Americans account for about 3 percent. Almost 9 percent of Washingtonians are Hispanic American.

Washington, D.C., Population 1950–2010

What factors might account for the recent increase in the population of Washington, D.C., after years of decline?

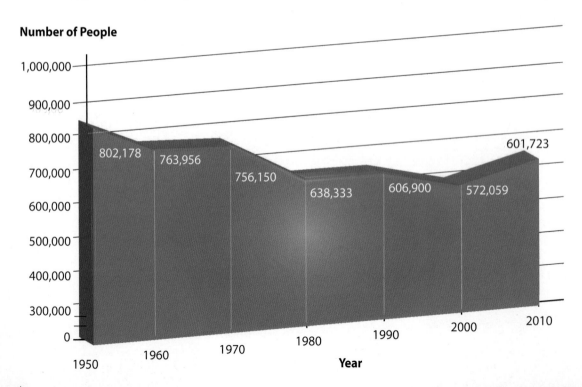

Number of People

802,178 · 763,956 · 756,150 · 638,333 · 606,900 · 572,059 · 601,723

1950 · 1960 · 1970 · 1980 · 1990 · 2000 · 2010

Year

A Chinese New Year parade is held annually in Washington's Chinatown neighborhood.

Washington is a bit smaller than Denver, Colorado, in population, and it is slightly larger than Las Vegas, Nevada.

Females make up a higher proportion of people in Washington than they do in the United States as a whole. They account for 53 percent of Washington's population, compared to roughly 51 percent for the nation.

People in Washington tend to be more educated than in the country overall. Among Washingtonians at least 25 years old, more than 48 percent have a bachelor's or higher degree, compared to approximately 28 percent for the country as a whole.

Every weekday, hundreds of thousands of people use the Metro to travel to and from work or get around the city.

Politics and Government

Washington is governed by a mayor and a 13-member city council. The mayor and council members are elected by the citizens of the district, but this was not always true. For more than 170 years, the mayor of Washington was chosen by the president of the United States. In 1973, the Home Rule Act gave district residents the right to vote for their mayor and city council. Still, the city's budget and all laws passed by the council must be approved by the U.S. Congress. The judges in the city's courts are appointed by the president, subject to approval by the U.S. Senate.

At the Capitol, members of Congress have a great deal of control over Washington's local government.

The Wilson Building is Washington's city hall.

Since Washington, D.C., is not a state, an important political issue for many residents is lack of **representation** in the federal government. It is only since 1961 that residents of Washington can vote in presidential elections. The District of Columbia has no U.S. senators. It sends one delegate to the House of Representatives, but that person cannot vote for or against legislation on the floor of the House. Although district residents must pay federal taxes and follow federal laws, they cannot help choose, in the same way as residents of states, the people who make those laws. Many car license plates in Washington carry the slogan "Taxation without Representation."

Washington's official song is called "Washington."

Here are the words to the song:

*Washington, the fairest city
    in the greatest land of all,
Named for one, our country's
    father, who first answered
    freedom's call,
God bless our White House,
    our Capitol too,
And keep ever flying the Red,
    White and Blue.*

*Grandest spot beneath the
    sun is Washington.*

*Oh, the cherry blossoms bring
    a lot of joy each Spring,
And the statue of Abe Lincoln
    greets your eye,
When parades pass in review
    down Pennsylvania Avenue,
Ev'rybody lifts their voices
    to the sky!*

*Grandest spot beneath the
    sun is Washington.*

Cultural Groups

A merican Indians were once the only people living in the area that is now Washington. By the time the District of Columbia was created, nearly all of them were gone. They were killed by disease or in battle, or they were driven from their lands by settlers of European heritage. Some of these settlers owned or bought slaves who were brought to North America from Africa.

A great many of the workers who built the White House and the Capitol were slaves. Today, African Americans make up more than half of Washington's residents. Every January, they remember their struggles for equal rights on the birthday of Martin Luther King, Jr. A wreath-laying ceremony at the Lincoln Memorial features local choirs, guest speakers, and a presentation of King's historic "I Have a Dream" speech. In February, events are held across the city to mark African American History Month. The DanceAfrica celebration in June features African dancing, concerts, and a marketplace.

Martin Luther King, Jr., gave his "I Have a Dream" speech to a huge crowd on the National Mall in 1963.

Held every year since 1971, the Saint Patrick's Day parade honors the Irish heritage of many Washingtonians.

Many Washingtonians trace their cultural **heritage** back to European countries. The annual St. Patrick's Day Parade features Irish dancers, musicians, and floats. In summer, the Festa Italiana offers authentic Italian food and street performances by strolling magicians and singers. Roasted lamb, **souvlaki**, and gyros are served at the Greek Festival in the fall, accompanied by music and lively Greek dancing.

People of Asian descent make up a small percentage of the district's residents, but they are an active part of the city's culture. Each January or February, Chinese New Year is celebrated with fireworks and a parade in Washington's Chinatown. A Japanese lantern-lighting ceremony is part of the yearly Cherry Blossom Festival. Fiesta Asia! is held each spring. Events typically include a parade, Korean martial arts demonstrations, Filipino dancing, Malaysian folk games, and more.

The annual Caribbean Carnival features a parade, traditional Caribbean foods, and crafts exhibits. Many marchers in the parade wear elaborate and colorful costumes.

Many Hispanic immigrants live in the Adams Morgan area in Washington's northwest quadrant. The area is actually one of Washington's most culturally diverse neighborhoods, with residents of African and Asian, as well as Latin American, heritage. It is known for its variety of international restaurants, active night life, and colorful murals.

Arts and Entertainment

Washington has movie theaters and music clubs where people can listen to rock, blues, jazz, or rap. But perhaps Washington's greatest entertainment feature is its amazing number and variety of museums.

The Smithsonian Institution is the most amazing of them all. Part of it is the National Air and Space Museum, where visitors can touch a piece of the Moon. The National Museum of Natural History and the National Zoo are also parts of the Smithsonian, as is the Museum of American History, which has been called "the national attic." Its collection includes a hat worn by Abraham Lincoln, a car owned by Elvis Presley, and a pair of ruby slippers worn by Judy Garland when she played the character of Dorothy in the movie *The Wizard of Oz*. The National Museum of the American Indian is also part of the Smithsonian, as are a number of art museums.

The annual Smithsonian Folklife Festival draws performers from around the world.

Many Washingtonians enjoy classical music concerts at the Kennedy Center for the Performing Arts.

One of the finest art collections in the world can be seen at the National Gallery of Art. The Newseum is a museum that is about reporting the news. Visitors learn about the history of journalism and the latest technology used in print and broadcast news. The U.S. Holocaust Memorial Museum is a memorial to the approximately 6 million people murdered by the Nazi government of Germany during World War II. Sharks and other types of fish, as well as turtles and eels, may be seen at the National Aquarium. At the "touch tank," visitors can handle some of the animals.

The John F. Kennedy Center for the Performing Arts has three main theaters. Music, opera, and ballet are performed there year-round. Plays are also staged there. The Folger Shakespeare Library is home to the world's largest collection of materials relating to William Shakespeare. Plays and concerts are given there as well. For two weeks each summer, the Smithsonian Folklife Festival is held outdoors on the Mall. It celebrates crafts, cooking, storytelling, music and other aspects of the traditional cultural heritage of countries around the globe.

Sports

Politics may be the biggest topic of conversation in Washington, but sports is very close behind. People in the city do not just talk about sports. They participate. The District of Columbia's parks are used by joggers, walkers, hikers, bicyclers, and horseback riders. Canoeists, kayakers, and many other boaters paddle, motor, and sail on the city's rivers. Golfers enjoy three public golf courses within the district.

Washington's Department of Parks and Recreation offers many chances for children and teenagers to get involved in sports. It sponsors programs in football, track and field, baseball, softball, basketball, boxing, soccer, and tennis.

For grown-ups, there are adult leagues in basketball, flag football, kickball, and softball. The city's several **aquatic** centers have programs for both adults and children. At these pools the city organizes swimming lessons, lifeguard training, competitive swim teams, and open swims.

In 2010, DC United's 17-year-old Andy Najar became Major League Soccer's youngest Rookie of the Year ever.

For those who like to watch professional sports, Washington offers many opportunities. The Washington Nationals baseball team and the Washington Wizards basketball team both play in the city. The Washington Redskins football team plays just outside it. The city also hosts the Washington Capitals hockey team and the DC United men's soccer team. The area has three professional women's teams as well. The Washington Mystics play basketball, the Washington Freedom play soccer, and the DC Divas play football. Washington hosts a professional tennis tournament every year.

The Potomac offers kayakers an opportunity to enjoy their sport against a background of national monuments.

The Washington Senators were the city's Major League Baseball team from 1901 to 1960. In 1961, the Senators moved away and became the Minnesota Twins. A new team called the Senators played in Washington from 1961 until 1971, when it became the Texas Rangers. The district was without a baseball team until 2005, when the Montreal Expos moved to town and became the Washington Nationals.

DC United, as of 2010, had won Major League Soccer's MLS Cup four times. That is more championships than any other team in the league.

Washington's Gallaudet University serves deaf students, who communicate with sign language. In the 1890s, the school's football team began the tradition of the football huddle in order to hide its signed play signals from opposing teams.

National Averages Comparison

The United States is a federal republic, consisting of fifty states and the District of Columbia. Alaska and Hawai'i are the only non-contiguous, or non-touching, states in the nation. Today, the United States of America is the third-largest country in the world in population. The United States Census Bureau takes a census, or count of all the people, every ten years. It also regularly collects other kinds of data about the population and the economy. How does the District of Columbia compare to the national average?

Comparison Chart

United States 2010 Census Data *	USA	District of Columbia
Admission to Union	NA	July 16, 1790
Land Area (in square miles)	3,537,438.44	61.40
Population Total	308,745,538	601,723
Population Density (people per square mile)	87.28	9,800.05
Population Percentage Change (April 1, 2000, to April 1, 2010)	9.7%	5.2%
White Persons (percent)	72.4%	38.5%
Black Persons (percent)	12.6%	50.7%
American Indian and Alaska Native Persons (percent)	0.9%	0.3%
Asian Persons (percent)	4.8%	3.5%
Native Hawaiian and Other Pacific Islander Persons (percent)	0.2%	0.1%
Some Other Race (percent)	6.2%	4.1%
Persons Reporting Two or More Races (percent)	2.9%	2.9%
Persons of Hispanic or Latino Origin (percent)	16.3%	9.1%
Not of Hispanic or Latino Origin (percent)	83.7%	90.9%
Median Household Income	$52,029	$58,553
Percentage of People Age 25 or Over Who Have Graduated from High School	80.4%	77.8%

*All figures are based on the 2010 United States Census, with the exception of the last two items. Percentages may not add to 100 because of rounding.

How to Improve My Community

Strong communities make strong states. Think about what features are important in your community. What do you value? Education? Health? Forests? Safety? Beautiful spaces? Government works to help citizens create ideal living conditions that are fair to all by providing services in communities. Consider what changes you could make in your community. How would they improve your state as a whole? Using this concept web as a guide, write a report that outlines the features you think are most important in your community and what improvements could be made. A strong state needs strong communities.

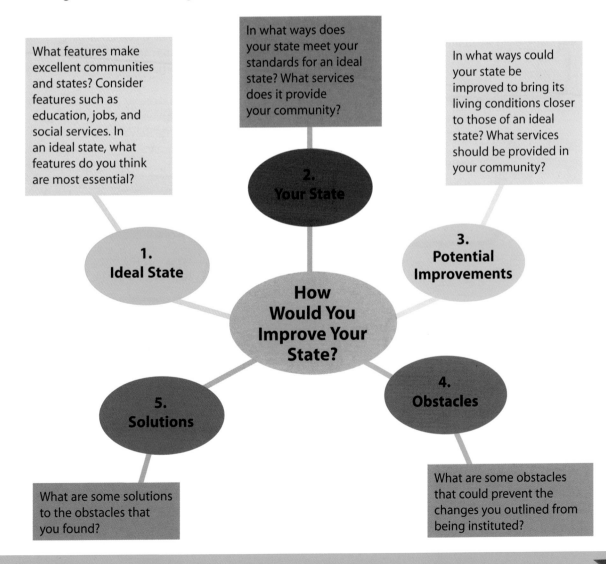

What features make excellent communities and states? Consider features such as education, jobs, and social services. In an ideal state, what features do you think are most essential?

In what ways does your state meet your standards for an ideal state? What services does it provide your community?

In what ways could your state be improved to bring its living conditions closer to those of an ideal state? What services should be provided in your community?

2. Your State

1. Ideal State

3. Potential Improvements

How Would You Improve Your State?

5. Solutions

4. Obstacles

What are some solutions to the obstacles that you found?

What are some obstacles that could prevent the changes you outlined from being instituted?

Exercise Your Mind!

Think about these questions and then use your research skills to find the answers and learn more fascinating facts about Washington, D.C. A teacher, librarian, or parent may be able to help you locate the best sources to use in your research.

1 How much snow falls in Washington in an average winter?

2 Where did Washington's celebrated cherry trees come from?

3 Of all the libraries in the world, which has the most books?

4 When did the U.S. government move to Washington?

5 What slogan about political rights is on many of Washington's car license plates?

6 What group of American Indians lived in the area that is now Washington when Europeans began to arrive?

a. The Mohawks
b. The Piscataway
c. The Atlanta Braves
d. The Potomacs

7 Who was the first president to live in the White House?

8 Who are Tian Tian and Mei Xiang?

Words to Know

aquatic: having to do with water

budget: a plan for money coming in and money being spent

compromise: settling a disagreement by each side giving up part of what it wants

federal: having to do with the national government of the United States

heritage: something handed down from the past, or the history and customs of a certain group

influence: the power or ability to change the behavior of a person or organization without using force

monument: a building or statue made to honor a person or event

piedmont: land at the foot of a mountain range

representation: standing in for someone else, such as what members of Congress do in speaking for the people who elected them

residents: the people who live in a specific place

souvlaki: a Greek dish made from pieces of lamb or other meat that are placed on a small stick, often with vegetables, and grilled

Index

Log on to www.av2books.com

AV[2] by Weigl brings you media enhanced books that support active learning. Go to www.av2books.com, and enter the special code found on page 2 of this book. You will gain access to enriched and enhanced content that supplements and complements this book. Content includes video, audio, web links, quizzes, a slide show, and activities.

Audio
Listen to sections of the book read aloud.

Video
Watch informative video clips.

Embedded Weblinks
Gain additional information for research.

Try This!
Complete activities and hands-on experiments.

WHAT'S ONLINE?

Try This!	Embedded Weblinks	Video	EXTRA FEATURES
Test your knowledge of the state in a mapping activity.	Discover more attractions in the District of Columbia.	Watch a video introduction to the District of Columbia.	**Audio** Listen to sections of the book read aloud.
Find out more about precipitation in your city.	Learn more about the history of the District of Columbia.	Watch a video about the features of the District of Columbia.	
Plan what attractions you would like to visit in the District of Columbia.	Learn the full lyrics of the official song of the District of Columbia.		**Key Words** Study vocabulary, and complete a matching word activity.
Learn more about the early natural resources of the District of Columbia.			**Slide Show** View images and captions, and prepare a presentation.
Write a biography about a notable resident of the District of Columbia.			
Complete an educational census activity.			**Quizzes** Test your knowledge.

AV[2] was built to bridge the gap between print and digital. We encourage you to tell us what you like and what you want to see in the future.

Sign up to be an AV[2] Ambassador at www.av2books.com/ambassador.